The Adventures of Frankie and Friends

A Sailing Adventure for the Awareness and Acceptance of Autism

BY TINA M. ROBBINS

Copyright © 2014 Tina M Robbins

All rights reserved.

ISBN: 1495397262

ISBN 13: 9781495397264

Library of Congress Control Number: 2014902463

CreateSpace Independent Publishing Platform

North Charleston, SC

For my four wonderful children—
you inspire me everyday.

TMR

Dear Parents and Educators,

The Frankie and Friends series was created as a tool to teach acceptance of all children with special needs and varying exceptionalities. Awareness begins at home and in the classroom environment as these are the two critical places where the mind of the child is molded. Frankie is a child that has been taught at a very young age that there are other children in the world that are different than he is and as he travels through his adventures, he not only will teach your children how to accept others but he will also bring awareness to varying disorders. The books give a child's perspective, assisted by the solid but simple teachings of his or her caregivers, on meeting and interacting with children who have disabilities. I hope you will find that once this book is read to a child, it will help him or her understand what makes a child extra special, and it will also make a difference in his or her future perspective of social acceptance. Let's make awareness an adventure, one child at time!

Hi, my name is Frankie, and I'm eight years old. I have brown hair, blue eyes, and really big ears—but that's OK.

My mom says I'm a curious boy, because I love to explore and pretend to be all different kinds of people. My mom teaches me a lot of important things. She says that when I go on my adventures in my make-believe world and in my real world, I must remember that everyone is different and special in his or her own way. She even says there are some extra-special boys and girls we must always be kind to. Do you know anyone who is extra special?

Sometimes I like to pretend to be a fisherman, an astronaut, or even a superhero. I never know whom I will meet during one of my adventures, but whoever it may be, he or she will have to be adventurous like me. Do you like to have pretend adventures?

Today I want to be a boat captain and sail the ocean, looking for treasures. Are you ready to come sailing with me?

I'm sailing toward Mystery Island, and there I'm looking for treasure chests full of gold. I may need to fight off pirates on my way. Will you help me?

I see the island ahead, and I have my treasure map ready to begin my search. Luckily, I don't see any pirates, but that's probably because they know I'm the mightiest ship captain in the world.

I drop my anchor on the edge of Mystery Island, and off in the distance I see a family playing in the sand around a fire. They could be islanders, so I must be careful not to tell them about my search for treasures.

As I get closer and begin to follow my map, I become more curious about the people I see ahead on the island. They look like my family, and there's a boy who looks to be about my age. I wonder if he would want to go on my treasure hunt with me.

The boy is sitting alone away from his mom and dad, and I decide to talk to him so I can find out his name. A co-captain might be helpful, and I could sure use help finding the treasures.

As I get closer to the boy, he seems to be talking to himself, maybe repeating some type of code. He doesn't look at me, but I sit down next to him and wait to get his attention. He is still not looking at me, but that's OK, because he must be thinking about something very important. Maybe he knows where the treasure chest is and doesn't know whether he should tell me.

"My name is Frankie," I say. "What's your name? Would you like to be my co-captain and help me find the treasures of Mystery Island?"

"My name is Andrew," the boy says, "and my brain is quicker than a lightning bolt. I can add four thousand digits at a time, and I don't really like pizza."

"OK, you can be my co-captain, Andrew, and if you want to come on my adventure, we can use your powers to find the treasures on my map."

"I have to tell my mom and dad first. I also need to feed my cat and finish the sand castle I started."

"I have an idea!" I say. "I will ask your mom if you can explore with me while you feed your cat and finish your sand castle."

"OK, I guess."

So I walk toward Andrew's mom, wondering if Andrew is a curious boy like me or if he is one of those extra-special people my mom has taught me about.

"Are you Andrew's mom?" I ask.

"Yes, I am," she says happily.

"My name is Frankie. Is it OK if Andrew comes exploring with me to look for the treasures of Mystery Island?"

"Yes, sure it is! But I just want to let you know that Andrew is an extra-special boy. He has autism, and he may not think or act exactly like you or me."

"Autism?" I ask.

"Yes," she says. "It is something that makes Andrew extra special and a little bit different than other children. Andrew's brain thinks in a different way from you and me, and sometimes it can look like he's not paying attention to you or not having fun."

She says, "There may be times when he won't look at you right in the eyes, or he may be speaking out loud to himself about something he is thinking in his brain. He may even sometimes not answer you, or he may decide to explore in a different direction."

"That's OK with me. Andrew will make a great co-captain, even though he is not exactly like me, because explorers need bright ideas and quick thinking to explore and find treasures."

As Andrew and I go exploring, we discover that we like a lot of the same games, books, and imaginary places. But there are times when he is hard to understand and doesn't really answer some of my questions. I don't mind, though, because like my mom said, we are all different in our own way, and he is a great co-captain.

We search Mystery Island and follow the map to the treasure location, but all we find is a pile of coconuts buried beneath the sand. There's no gold! This must have been a treasure for the Coconut Hunter, but it was fun looking for it anyway.

Andrew and I laugh at our silly, imaginary adventure, and it is soon time for me to go home.

"Why are you going?" Andrew asks. "I mean, thank you for asking me to play with you and be your co-captain. It was fun looking for buried treasure, but I do think I was the better treasure hunter, so maybe next time I should be captain."

I think my new friend, Andrew, who has autism, is special. I understand he doesn't mean to hurt any feelings with his words, so I tell him, "Next time, you can definitely be captain."

I say farewell to my new friend, Andrew, who has autism, and sail back to my house.

When I get home, my mom asks me how my day has been, and I tell her that I sailed the ocean blue as a ship captain in search of treasures. When she asks me whether I found any treasures, I tell her that I certainly did. His name is Andrew, and he has autism. He is one of those special people she taught me about. Andrew has a brain that is quicker than a lightning bolt. He can add four thousand digits at one time, and he doesn't like pizza.

My mom smiles and says how lucky I am to have found such a wonderful treasure.

THE END

ABOUT THE AUTHOR
TINA M. ROBBINS

Tina M. Robbins is a new childrens' author. Mrs. Robbins graduated in 1994 with a Bachelors Degree in Psychology from Florida State University and from St. Thomas University School of Law in 1997 with a Juris Doctor degree. Mrs. Robbins enjoyed her primary career as a Family Law litigator with a special interest in domestic cases involving special needs children. In 2012, Mrs. Robbins retired her career as a litigator to concentrate on rearing her children and advocating for their needs. Mrs. Robbins lives in Central Florida, is married and has four wonderful children. Zachary, 14, is her oldest son and is her only child without disabilities but creative and academically brilliant. Sarah, 13 is her most severely handicapped child born with a brain disorder causing failure to speak and cognitive delays. Sarah also suffers from Transverse Myelitis causing paralysis from waist down. Charlie, 8, is her third child who was diagnosed with Autism and ADHD at the age of 5 but thriving with adaptations. Jeremy, 6, is her fourth child diagnosed with ADHD and Oppositional Defiance Disorder at the age of 4. Mrs. Robbins loves to cook, travel and fundraise.

CPSIA information can be obtained
at www.ICGtesting.com
Printed in the USA
BVHW012009200323
660808BV00001B/1